MW00810202

What I Believe

REBEKAH MERCER

WHAT I BELIEVE

BOOKS

New York · London

Contents

Introduction

In the second book of his *Nicomachean Ethics*, Aristotle warned of the challenges of those with means when donating to those less fortunate or in need: "To give away money is an easy matter and in any one's power. But to decide to whom to give it and how large and when, and for what purpose and how, is neither in every one's power nor an easy matter."

Philanthropy certainly is not an easy matter – or maybe in some ways it can become too easy a matter. Even well-meaning traditionalists can wreak havoc by unrestricted and untargeted giving to universities and foundations that can quite unapologetically use such largess for agendas never dreamed of by well-meaning benefactors, and quite injurious to the public good.

In contemporary America, we confront a philanthropic paradox: many conservatives who have done well, given the private enterprise system and the security ensured by traditional American values, generously endow universities where liberal orthodoxy dominates and often insists that financial success is not a reflection of American soundness, but of personal and national pathology. Non-profits, especially in education and the arts, thereby often feel free to use bequests in the opposite fashion from which they were intended – almost as if to provide an unsolicited psychological penance for the donor.

So, philanthropy – "a love of mankind" – can be either a great good or something quite different. The choice depends entirely on the intellect, knowledge, ethics, good will, and hard work of the donor to ensure that a targeted institution is empowered to help, rather than to corrupt, others and itself in the process.

The generosity of Rebekah Mercer, along with her sisters, Jennifer and Heather, and her parents, Robert and Diana, has never been indifferent or haphazard. Instead, their giving is engaged, principled, and knowledgeable –

and aimed at ensuring that each ensuing generation of Americans can have the continued freedom to live under a unique constitutional order as envisioned by the original framers who founded the nation.

Rebekah Mercer is currently unapologetic about concluding that America is now at a great crossroads, in which we are nearing the logical limits of progressivism from Illinois to California to New York. The common strains at the state, local, and federal level are a war on the middle class; unsustainable entitlements; a new chauvinistic tribalism euphemistically known as identity politics; restrictions on free expression on our campuses; open borders that along with a new global gospel, erode our sovereignty; and unelected deep-state bureaucracies that use their enormous powers of surveillance, regulation, and deep pockets to target individuals deemed dangerous to the idea of an omnipotent and redistributive government.

Rebekah Mercer and her family see philanthropy neither as an investment in the Mercer name nor as a pile-on to trendy or popular agendas. Indeed, many of Rebekah's charitable contributions are hardly known to the public and often directed at less well-known but essential causes, individuals, and institutions. But her reticence to avoid public attention does not mean she is anonymous. Rebekah is more than ready to defend her family, her vision, and her activism when provoked. And she has been absolutely resolute when challenged, defamed, and smeared.

Rebekah Mercer's generosity *is* branded – by the multitude of different ways it promotes and invests in constitutional and limited government, the rule of law, due process, free speech and expression, and the rights of an individual against an often bullying state – more or less a catalogue of the very titles that Roger Kimball routinely publishes at Encounter Books. At no time in my memory have those values been more sacred – and yet under assault as we have so recently witnessed, from the shouting down of guest speakers at college campuses, to the recent

U.S. Senate confirmation hearings on the nomination of Supreme Court nominee and later Justice Brett Kavanaugh.

What empowers Rebekah Mercer's giving is her near mathematic precision – characteristic of a Stanford university mathematics and engineering systems graduate – with which she investigates beneficiaries. Like all of her family, she does not privilege the received wisdom of the status quo – given how often in error it has been today and in the past. Instead, she is Socratic in questioning the why, how, when, and where her contributions can make a difference – and whether anticipated results justify generous investments.

Her engagement and research into the causes she supports are also reflective of her own nurturing and home-schooling of her four children. I have gotten to know her children. They are not just prodigies, but kind, engaged, and ethical young citizens – in other words, they too are the lucky recipients of Rebekah's generosity and love of all things human.

For all these reasons and far more it is all

our great honor to introduce to you this year's recipient of the Encounter Prize for Advancing American Ideals, the esteemed Ms. Rebekah Mercer.

VICTOR DAVIS HANSON

The Hoover Institution,
and Chair of the Encounter Committee
of The Bradley Foundation

WHAT I BELIEVE

Remarks given at the Encounter Books
Twentieth Anniversary Gala

OCTOBER 11, 2018

I AM GRATEFUL

to receive an award bearing the words "American ideals." I am privileged to be an American, but more than privileged, I am thankful to be an American.

America is a miracle and a blessing. Its birth, the fusing of thirteen independent colonies into a new nation, following a victory over King George, ruler of the greatest military power on earth, is the social and political equivalent of the rarest of celestial syzygies.

With the Revolutionary War already underway, our Founding Fathers, and other delegates to the Second Continental Congress, met in Philadelphia in 1776 to debate the goals of – and to explain the justification for – the hostilities between the American patriots and the British Crown. Drawing on ideals and principles from the Bible, from the ancient classics, and from some of their European contemporaries – especially John Locke – they created, primarily by the hand of Thomas Jefferson, one of the most eloquent, revolutionary, and consequential documents in human history: The Declaration of Independence.

Eleven years later, with the Revolutionary War settled in favor of the patriots, a group of our founders, edited by the hand of fate, returned to Philadelphia under the auspices of a constitutional convention, with the announced purpose of amending the Articles of Confederation, but with the final result of replacing it – root and branch – with a new framework: the Constitution of the United States of America.

These two documents, the Declaration of Independence and the Constitution of the United States of America, crystallized the creed of a rugged, resourceful people;

A people who valued self-reliance and personal responsibility over dependence on government;

A people who recognized that, in a country unleashed from the hierarchies and regimentation of the Old World, anyone could chart his own course and be assured that he himself was solely responsible for his success or for his failure.

On the anvil of these two documents, our forefathers forged the freest, most prosperous, and most powerful nation in human history. The ideals of federalism, limited representative government, free market capitalism, inalienable rights, private property, due process, sound money and Equality for All before the bench of a blind and impartial Justice unleashed the human imagination as never before in human history.

Courageous men and women from around the world, yearning to be free, flooded America's shores eager to join our great experiment.

And what is the state of that experiment today?

"Now we are engaged in a great civil war," said Abraham Lincoln at Gettysburg in 1863.

One hundred and fifty-five years later, it is barely hyperbolic to echo the Great Emancipator.

We are not yet in armed conflict, but we are facing an ever more belligerent, frantic, and absurd group of radicals in a struggle for the soul of our country. How did we get to this point?

In 1938, Huey Long, governor of Louisiana, responding to the question, "Do you think we will ever have fascism in America?" replied, "Sure, only we'll call it anti-fascism."

Today, this is the reality. Antifa, one of the militant arms of our current domestic foes, is intent on strangling our freedoms in the name of a belief system that, in the twentieth century, was responsible for the deaths of 100 million people.

One wonders how any intelligent, well-educated individual could be attracted to Antifa. How could he fail to appreciate the astonishing, wonder-working power of America's founding principles, especially when recent world history provides so many festering illustrations of the evils of dictator-led command economies: China under Mao, Cuba under Castro, Venezuela under Chavez and now Maduro, and, of course, the Soviets under just about any of their various and variously disguised tyrants.

Progressives in America have spent the last five or six decades insinuating themselves into the fabric of the American education system. They've taken to heart the lessons of Antonio Gramsci in their long campaign against our institutions and have obtained almost complete dominion over education, perhaps our most effective tool for directing the future of our country.

Alexander the Great was not afraid of an army of lions being led by a lamb; but he did fear an army of lambs being led by a lion.

Each imagining himself to be the lion that will one day conquer the American states and the psyches of their citizens, the progressives have been remodeling the American education system to churn out wave upon wave of ovine zombies steeped in the anti-American myths of the radical left, ignorant of basic civics, economics, and history, and unfit for critical thinking.

Theirs has been a challenging task, difficult to complete within the constraints of a K through 12 education and made yet more challenging because the students return home at the end of each school day where they're exposed to the common-sense attitudes and influence of their irksome bourgeois parents. What to do?

College! Yes, college. What a great idea! Students don't go home for months at a time. They eat on the campus. They sleep on the campus. But wait! Tuition is expensive. Let's make tuition free! But wait! College is hard, and the state primary and secondary education apparatus is exceptional in failing to prepare its graduates to enter any institution of higher learning.

The solution: stuff the university curriculum with politicized or otherwise inane courses that anyone can pass. The list is endless, and you can spend an entire day laughing about the silly courses and the level of partisanship. Here are a few that might leave you gobsmacked: Tree Climbing, Cornell University – "Climbing course will teach you how to get up into the canopy of any tree, to move around, even to climb from one tree to another without touching the ground." One wonders just where the provost grew up to view this as an acceptable course at an institution where the yearly cost exceeds $60,000 per student. Then there is "The Sociology of Miley Cyrus: Race, Class, Gender, and Media," Skidmore College. The professor described it as "a rigorous way of looking at what's relevant about sociology." No doubt!

Other stimulating (and hard to flunk) classes include "West World, Our World," "The Art of Walking," and "How to Watch Television."

Added to these pitifully absurd classes, are the "*fill-in-the-blank* studies" majors, which are nothing more than unapologetic courses in activism. We call the graduates of these curricula "Snowflakes." Almost any word or topic mentioned in their presence requires a trigger warning so that they will have a chance to pop in their earbuds and crank the volume on their iPhones so as not to be offended.

But beyond the Snowflakes, most serious students find many of the academic courses in the humanities to be profoundly antagonistic towards American ideals and the American experiment. Some boldly declare the United States to be an evil country playing the role of master villain on the world stage, whether in terms of its foreign policy or in terms of its domestic industry.

That America is an imperialist exploiter is a pernicious, foolish, and ignorant view – informed not by history but by the malignant ideology of the likes of Antifa and the totalitarian enemies of humanity that have come to power over the course of the last century and that, even today is responsible for the suffering of hundreds of millions of people.

This toxic interpretation of America has gradually oozed out of the confines of the college campuses, oiling its way into our culture at large and, most egregiously, into our mainstream news media.

Our Founding Fathers saw the press as a de facto fourth branch of government, indispensable in holding our elected officials accountable and acting as a watchdog to protect our freedoms.

Thomas Jefferson argued that, "The only security of all is in a free press. The force of public opinion cannot be resisted when permitted freely to be expressed."

The mainstream media today has neither the vitality nor the integrity to play the role that Jefferson described for it two centuries ago. Today, journalists of the mainstream media are little more than the Machiavellian foot soldiers of the progressive left, unethical to their very hearts, shameless about writing lies and defaming people, and assiduously filtering the stories they print through a prism of partisan prejudice.

I know just how unethical, deranged, and shameless some of these journalists really are because I have personal experience as a target for their defamatory fantasies and slanders.

It's just business as usual that the alleged drinking habits of a college student from decades ago are put under a microscope for review while the self-admitted use of hard drugs by the most recently retired Commander in Chief is pounced on as an opportunity to praise him and to point out how he had experienced much and knew much because of his criminal drug use.

Similarly, the domestic abuse allegations

against Keith Ellison, the current DNC chair and candidate for Attorney General of Minnesota are swept under the rug. Justice Kavanaugh, on the other hand (and it is *Justice* Kavanaugh), was tried and convicted on the editorial pages of America's major broadsheets with uncorroborated accusations in place of evidence.

The left knows that a Supreme Court dominated by judges who respect the original intent of our Constitution, and who recognize that their role is to determine the constitutionality of existing legislation rather than to craft new legislation themselves, poses an existential threat to the progressive agenda, and so the journalists have united in an attempt to destroy Justice Kavanaugh at any cost.

Joining forces with these partisan journalists, and the pied pipers and peddlers of the Snowflake curricula in academia, is the great majority of Hollywood and the cream of Silicon Valley, which, having risen to the pinnacle of technical and financial power, is now curdling in Peter-principle fashion as it seeks its next promotion.

Together these form an effective and magnificently funded coalition, a coalition of progressives with an agenda intent on transforming America and driving her far from her founding ideals.

It is a testament to the will and wisdom of the American people and to the boiling over of their anger that, despite the enormous power and wealth of this coalition, America's voice can still be heard and, against all odds, Donald J. Trump replaced Barack Obama in the Oval Office in 2017, leaving Hillary Clinton to splutter hysterical and alone on the sidelines of history.

You have probably noticed that it is all too often the most privileged of Americans, those who have been educated at the most prestigious universities, those who have been the most blessed by America's bounty, who have the greatest scorn for America and for her ideals.

The Founding Fathers, and later the pioneers who tamed the American wilderness, and still later the men and women who fought and died in world wars to preserve Western civilization, were proud and self-reliant. Sadly, many of their descendants now see themselves and one another either as victims entitled to wallow in grievances or as victimizers compelled to apologize endlessly for actions for which they bear no responsibility.

Too many Americans today have not been taught and have never learned the pivotal importance of the First Amendment. Its purpose is not to protect the people who are saying things that you like, but to protect the people who are saying things that you don't like. Without it, anything intolerable to even the most delicate of Snowflakes becomes hate speech. Jefferson warned us that freedom of speech "cannot be limited without being lost."

Young and clueless Americans wear t-shirts emblazoned with the likenesses of Che Guevara and other enemies of freedom even as they tear down statues of American heroes without whose sacrifices they might be living in poverty and pestilence.

And today it has become common among the *bien pensant* to sneer at hard working, law abiding, patriotic Americans while sentimentalizing illegal immigrants and faux refugees – even when the aliens in question are felons or aspiring or actual terrorists who proudly proclaim their hatred for America.

We have reached the point that, in the words of the brilliant Thomas Sowell, "We have demonized those who produce, subsidized those who refuse to produce, and canonized those who complain."

None of these tragic situations could be more distant from the ideals that have defined and animated our great nation throughout its existence. And none of them could be more dangerous to the preservation and propagation of those ideals.

I marvel at the rare privilege of being an American, but am acutely aware that a sacred obligation walks hand in hand with that privilege – an obligation to champion American ideals, to defend our Constitution, and both to shine the cleansing light of public disclosure on the corruption in government and to hold accountable those feckless invertebrates in elected office who, having sworn a sacred oath to defend it, willfully disregard the plain words of our Constitution.

The disrespect our elected officials have shown our Constitution over more than a century, has allowed government to mushroom to a size inconceivable to our founders.

Article 1, Section 10 of our Constitution says, in part, that: "No State shall [...] make any Thing but gold and silver Coin a Tender in Payment of Debts."

In 1971, Richard Nixon, perfecting the curse cast by the creation of the Federal Reserve in 1913, silenced the last fading echo of the gold standard. Since then, our lack of sound money and fiscal transparency has resulted, among other travesties, in the accrual of a national debt of $21.5 trillion dollars and counting (which doesn't even include the very much greater debt due to our unfunded liabilities). Congress has swapped our children's future and our children's children's future for a chance at re-election today.

Congressmen wrestle for the powers of office, but duck and dodge the responsibilities that go with it. And so, they have laid off their constitutionally mandated power of the purse and many of the responsibilities that accompany it to massive, un-elected, inept, and ineffective bureaucracies. The American people have yet to discover how to hold these bureaucratic behemoths to account.

The 10th Amendment to our Constitution was designed by our founders as an emergency brake to the accumulation of centralized power. Our Founding Fathers knew that too much power concentrated in too few hands, isolated from most of the country's population, would corrode the mechanisms of government and drag us inexorably into corruption.

Power must be kept as close to the people as possible and the citizens must be engaged and informed so as to hold their elected officials accountable.

As Aristotle warned the Greeks, if you choose to remain ignorant, you are destined to be ruled by tyrants. Indeed, remaining ignorant is a luxury we can ill afford if we are to retain our freedoms.

I am devoted to citizen engagement, to transparency in government, and to accountability for our elected representatives. I am unalterably opposed to entrenched and corrupt political interests in any corner of the political landscape. I believe in citizen government as our founders envisioned it, not in government by the career politician, not in politicians who barter away our freedoms for another term in office, not in politicians who ignore our Constitution, enrich themselves off of us taxpayers, and relentlessly expand their own powers while shirking their responsibilities.

These positions have left me the target of derision, slander, and enmity, especially from the unhinged left. "Rebekah Mercer wants to blow it all up," lies one journalist. "Mercer is dangerous," lies another. Mercer is a "Science Denier" proclaims the ridiculous *New York Times*. The shockingly unethical fantasist, Jane Mayer, tried to top them all with her ludicrous yarn, "A Parlor Game at Rebekah Mercer's Has No Get Out of Jail Free Card." But surely the award for most petty and ignorant demonization must go to an article published by *Politico* magazine about a bakery my sisters and I owned: "Trump Megadonor Rebekah Mercer Makes Terrible Cookies." I have to admit that I don't read most of the lies and nonsense, but this last article was brought to my attention by a friend who forwarded it to me with a note saying, "Who knew politics could also poison taste buds."

The nastiness in the media that has resulted from the philanthropic activity and civic engagement of my family and me is astounding. It has led to hate mail and protests in front of my home where several participants suggested I should suffer the fate of Marie Antoinette. Well, let them cast their stones. Let them impugn my motives in the most cynically ignorant manner. Let them issue their death threats.

I will not be silenced.

And I am comforted by the wisdom of Bette Davis, who said, "It's a sign of your worth, sometimes, if you're hated by the right people." Of course, I'm sure that she meant "by the left people."

Or as Charles MacKay put it in one of my favorite poems: "You have no enemies, you say? Alas! My friend, the boast is poor."

So, I wear their enmity with honor, and, in the meantime, I raise my children with a reverence, gratitude, and understanding for the cornucopia of blessings that is America. I homeschool them to educate them properly about history, economics, philosophy, and civics, to name a few vital areas of now arcane knowledge. In an age when American values are disparaged, and their protectors routinely depicted as villains, bigots, and sowers of hate, it is more vital than ever to speak up for those values and to pass them on to our children. The future of this precious land and the future of our progeny, depend upon it.

I'm so grateful to Encounter for what they do every day to ensure that we pass along the sacred knowledge and appreciation for America's founding principles.

As Ronald Reagan pointed out, "Freedom is never more than one generation away from extinction. We didn't pass it to our children in the bloodstream. It must be fought for, protected, and handed on for them to do the same."

Thomas Jefferson put it more succinctly when he said, "The price of freedom is eternal vigilance." I thank you for being here this evening and I hope that you will, please, join me in remaining eternally vigilant.

First American edition published in 2019 by Encounter Books, an activity of Encounter for Culture and Education, Inc., a nonprofit, tax exempt corporation. Encounter Books website address: www.encounterbooks.com

Manufactured in the United States and printed on acid-free paper. The paper used in this publication meets the minimum requirements of ANSI/NISO z39.48–1992 (R 1997) (*Permanence of Paper*).

FIRST AMERICAN EDITION

LIBRARY OF CONGRESS CATALOGING-IN-PUBLICATION DATA IS AVAILABLE